The Homeschool Guide

Everything you need to know for successfully homeschooling your children!

Table of Contents

Introduction

I want to thank you and congratulate you for downloading the book, *"The Homeschool Guide"*.

This book contains helpful information about homeschooling, and what you need to consider when deciding to homeschool.

Deciding to homeschool is a huge decision to make, and requires a lot of thought, effort and time. This book will explain to you many of the positives, along with some of the negatives associated with homeschooling.

You will learn what things you need to do before beginning to teach your child, how to prepare, and how to give your child the attention they require.

Homeschooling is not for everyone, but for some children and parents it can be highly beneficial. Hopefully, after reading this book you'll be clear on your decision to homeschool, and have the necessary tools available to do so successfully!

This book will explain to you tips and techniques that will allow you to successfully teach your children, and give them the best education possible!

Good luck with your homeschooling journey!

Chapter 1: Deciding to Homeschool

Are you thinking of homeschooling your child?

Deciding to homeschool your child should not be taken lightly. You need to consider a lot of things including your time and resources. While it may seem very difficult, the reward you and your child can receive outweighs it. As long as you can read and write, you can supervise your child's learning.

Homeschooling has been around for centuries. It was, however, between the 1970's and 80's that the term actually meant as an alternative way to educate a child. This happened after parents started questioning whether the public education system or private institutions were right for their child. They began wondering whether they could do a better job instead. This led to them taking the opportunity to become their child's teacher. Fortunately, it brought positive results, and soon, other parents were doing it too.

In recent times, the number of homeschooled children has grown, with an increase of around 11% each year over the last few years. While becoming your child's own teacher may seem intimidating, you educational background is not a hindrance at all. It has been proven that even parents without a high school degree can effectively teach their child. This feat is made possible with the help of programs intended to guide both parents and their children in their homeschooling. State laws and regulations on homeschooling have also made adjustments to make sure the education and safety of the child is met more effectively. These rules ensure that as a parent and teacher, you are providing your child with the education they need.

Benefits of Homeschooling

Homeschooling can provide families who give it a chance a positive effect in their academic, social, emotional, and spiritual growth. Research has shown how children who are homeschooled often outdo the majority of their peers who attends either public or private schools. This is because parents are able to provide their child with one-on-one learning, and additional attention they wouldn't receive through the conventional school system. It has also allowed parents to guide their child more and eliminate certain stress-factors that may hinder learning.

Academic Benefit

The one-on-one learning system helps the child to grasp ideas more effectively and according to their own speed. They don't have to worry about being left behind or having to wait on a classmate before the whole class can proceed to the next topic. A lesson can be repeated or advanced according to the child's learning speed.

Learning assimilation is made more effective with their study's time flexibility. A child can rest when needed and do other activities when they feel like it, given parental permission. Both parent and child can set a weekly study schedule to follow. They can work it out and adjust it according to what fits them best.

Social Benefits

One of the worries parents face today is their child's safety. As a homeschooler, your child is kept safer from such threats. A break-in at the school is one example you may save your child from. You will also avoid bullies who may cause your child harm.

Alcohol and drugs are another threat to your child's welfare. Many kids are found guilty of consuming these nearby school grounds. According to a study conducted by the National Center of Substance Abuse, 5 million teens indulge in drinking alcohol once a month. This becomes more disturbing for those under the legal age. Any teen drinking at the age of fifteen is more likely to be an alcoholic than a person who started drinking after reaching legal age.

By homeschooling your child, you can protect them from any social threat. You may help select the people they befriend, and have a strong influence in the groups they associate with.

Emotional Benefits

Emotional growth is one aspect of homeschooling that can be benefited by both child and parents. One of the most disturbing situations both wish to be free from is bullying. While it can harm the child physically, it does more emotionally.

Bullies threaten a child's emotional growth by humiliating them. If your child appears different (smart or with special needs) compared to their classmates, there's a chance they will be bullied. This negative input puts stress on your child. It can also makes them think they need to be like the rest of their classmates to be accepted. Eventually this can lead to your child giving in to peer-pressure, and doing things against their regular moral judgment.

Homeschool removes your child from the threat of being bullied. In addition, they get to spend more time with the family, where emotional needs can be better met. Providing your child the attention they need through learning, helps strengthen their bond with the family. Studies show that siblings who are taking homeschooling at the same time tend to be more helpful with each other.

Spiritual Benefits

The home is the best environment for spiritual training. As you bond with your child through homeschooling, you can choose to teach religious education if you please.

Reasons behind Homeschooling

When do you know your child needs to be homeschooled?

Parents usually decide on homeschooling their children believing they can do a better job. And it fact, those who attend school at home can do much better than their peers who attend regular classes. This doesn't disregard social growth.

While there are some people who believe deciding to homeschool your child is cutting their social growth, this is not always the case. If you ensure the child has interaction with other people often, and belongs to extracurricular groups, they can become well socialized, and develop strong interpersonal skills.

Before choosing to homeschool your child, you need to evaluate the reason why your family wants to do it. While excellent education is may be on top of the list, you need to determine exactly your ultimate goal behind your decision. Homeschooling is a large commitment for both you and your child. You need to be certain it is the right choice for you, your child, and your family. To help you, here are common reasons parents choose to homeschool their child.

The child has special needs regular schools can't provide for.

Whether your child has a learning disability or is sick, it is best to have the family support their education through homeschool. This will allow the child to continue their studies according to their learning speed and physical needs.

With homeschool, there is no pressure for slowing down the whole class nor pressure to understand everything straight away. Some children tend to lie about understanding what the teacher taught, fearing that their classmates will make fun of them.

The child's career is taking more time than school.

Children with careers, either in athletics, in the entertainment industry or similar can have a difficult time keeping up with regular classes.

Homeschooling allows them to be present in their career activities while learning academics.

Parents are concerned over their child's welfare.

With the news constantly focused on bullying and violence, parents can be afraid for their children's safety. This is why some choose to have their children homeschooled instead.

Bullying is a threat all parents wish to save their child from. Homeschooling can allow parents to protect them from it. They get to oversee their online activities and guide them in their social activities.

Parents want to have a stronger bond with their child.

There are parents who just want to have a stronger connection with their child. With homeschooling, they get to bond more.

Parents want to include religious learning.

Public schools don't always include religious classes. With homeschooling their child, parents are able to provide spiritual lessons.

The child wants to be homeschooled.

There are instances when a child decides to be homeschooled. Children who ask for it are self-motivated and are able to see their potential and their direction in a certain field.

Parents have jobs that require them to travel a lot.

Jobs that require parents to move around can disrupt the child's school attendance. While it may be okay to have them stay behind, this can affect how the child develops a relationship with their parents. If the child is very young, it is best to be with the parent.

Homeschooling also provides the child the chance to travel with their parents without jeopardizing academics.

Deciding to have your child homeschooled is not easy. The

whole family has a lot of adjustments to make both in their schedules and budget. Regardless of the many challenges in homeschooling, the rewards can be worth it.

In the next chapters, you will learn how to begin your homeschooling journey, and determine some homeschool goals that will make it a more fun and engaging experience for both you and your child.

Chapter 2: Learning More about Homeschool

If you are seriously looking at the possibility of having your child homeschooled, there are certain factors you need to consider. As was said in the previous chapter, choosing to homeschool is a big step to take. To start effectively, and help you through it, you need to learn more about homeschool.

Homeschooling Sources to Avoid

Be very wary when asking for homeschool advice. There are some organizations who may feed parents with narrow and negative ideas about homeschooling. They can even ask you to pay a large fee for membership and information. Here are some examples of groups and organization you might want to avoid.

Local Schools

It is their interest to keep you tied up to their school. To do this there's a chance they will misinform you about homeschooling. They may also be supportive in your choice, however, it can pay to be wary.

Distance learning programs

Distance learning programs can sometimes throw you off course in your aim of giving your child the best education. While there are many good programs, there will also be programs that are overpriced, and not up to a good standard.

Self-proclaimed homeschool experts

Be careful whom you will ask for advice. While there are many individuals who can give good information on how to start your homeschool, there will be those that will warn against it for no apparent reason.

Research Your Options

Believe it or not, researching about homeschooling is actually very easy. You can either learn about it for free or by paying a few dollars for resources. Here are the best sources that can help you know more about homeschooling.

Homeschool magazines and books

Magazines and books about homeschooling will educate you about how this system works and how you can work it more effectively. They provide you with insight and updates on what schools, programs, and the state says about it. These will keep you updated with the current trends and activities in the homeschooling world.

Homeschooling support groups and associations

Homeschooling support groups and associations will help you learn more about homeschooling, and will allow you to socialize with like-minded people.

Local homeschooling support groups are composed of families that meet on a regular basis. They can help you understand more about homeschool and how the state implements it. Some state regulations require parents to submit a report of their child's progress.

State level associations have membership fees. They can give you updates and invitations on various activities such as conferences or campouts. They will also provide you with information regarding recent changes on homeschooling state laws.

You can easily locate groups and associations by searching online.

Homeschooling conferences

Homeschooling conferences tend to happen every season.

Search for 'homeschooling events calendar' to find when these will be held and how to register. Most of these conferences also have curriculum fairs and catalogs which you and your child can review and try.

The Homeschool and Your State

When it comes to getting informed, you need to research how your state approaches homeschooling. Each state has a different requirement for families. Depending on the child's needs, the state may require parents to report their child's progress or submit to visitations. This is to ensure the child's welfare and their learning.

State associations can provide you with the information you need concerning your state's laws on homeschooling. You can also normally view this information online.

Setting Your Budget

Starting your homeschool requires you to set a budget for it. This will cover your curricula, textbooks, and even field trips. Other activities and tools may be needed such as your monthly internet, and subscription to additional homeschooling services.

Make a list of everything you may need. Expect your first year of homeschooling your child to be very expensive. You may need to buy items such as a blackboard, a study table, baskets for certain learning items, and other stuff you may use to organize your study space.

You might even consider tutors in the long run. For a higher level of learning, you have the option of hiring a tutor who can help your child learn more. You should also set a budget for you and your child's fieldtrips

Studying about homeschool before you engage in it can help you to start it more effectively, and save some money. Learn as much as you before you begin to ensure you are fully prepared.

Chapter 3: Determining Your Homeschool Goals

An important part of starting your homeschool is determining your goals.

Having bigger goals will help you set your smaller term goals. It will also help you see areas where your child needs to concentrate more. This will determine the activities you can do for the year to make their learning more effective.

Pitfalls of Homeschooling

Before we proceed to how you can effectively set your goals, familiarize yourself first with some of the potential the pitfalls of homeschooling.

Isolation

When your child opts for homeschool, this means they will be having their very own class. They won't have classmates (except for siblings) to study with.

One of the worries some people see in homeschooling is the isolation you will be giving the child. Many people believe this will make them less sociable. This is a real issue if you don't participate in groups regularly. Your child may not learn proper social skills, struggle with team work and find it difficult to make friends. Fortunately, this does not have to be a problem. There are groups formed for parents who homeschooled their child. You need to successfully form bonds with them, plan trips with them, and have activities your children will surely enjoy with other homeschoolers.

Committing to an advanced curriculum

Your child has their own speed of learning. If it's your first time to homeschool your child then try to stick to a curriculum that fits what they presently know. Not choosing a suitable curriculum can leave your child confused and frustrated with their learning.

The need to study the lessons

As you go through homeschool, you need to adjust your schedule. This is not just to provide your child the attention they need during homeschooling. You also need to study the lessons you are teaching. Other than studying, you also need to check, assess, and create a report of your child's progress. There is a lot more work involved than some may think.

Three Learning Domains

Determining goals is also about planning your lessons to meet them. Just like with classroom lessons, you need to meet the three domains of learning: cognitive, affective, and psychomotor.

- *Cognitive*

Cognitive learning means mental learning. This involves recall and retention of facts, concepts and patterns.

- *Affective*

Affective learning includes how we deal with our emotions such as values, appreciation, motivations, and attitudes.

- *Psychomotor*

Psychomotor deals with physical movements. These are motor skills and coordination which are measured by speed, precision, and distance.

Like any teacher, you should be able to ensure your child's growth in these three domains. Your yearly learning goals should contain these three.

Homeschooling Methods

To meet your yearly learning goals for your child, there are homeschooling methods you can use.

- *Traditional method*

The traditional method lets you set your curriculum and activities just like how a regular school does, complete with its traditional grading system.

- *Charlotte Mason method*

British educator, Charlotte Mason, developed an education approach centered on the child's atmosphere, discipline, and life.

- *Classical Education method*

The classical method is based on Dorothy Sayer's essay "The Lost Tool of Learning"

- *Montessori method*

The Montessori method deals with the concept that learning is a natural, self-directed process.

- *Eclectic method*

Eclectic method takes bits from the different homeschooling methods.

- *Unschooling*

Unschooling, or child led learning, is a common approach to homeschooling.

Planning Your Goals

How do you see your child ten years from now? Each year you must be working towards the ultimate education goal. You and your child's goals determine what your yearly study plan will be about.

Once you have your long-term goal set, it's time to determine your yearly steps. To help you know what your homeschool year should involve, here are ways to help you out.

1. Evaluate your child's previous performance.

If your child went to a regular school before deciding to homeschool, ask your teachers about their performance. Of course, you should also evaluate your child's behavior and attitude towards learning to really meet a specific goal. Remember, the number one reason why parents opt for homeschool is because they believe they can do a better job than schools.

If your child hasn't attended any schooling then you can base your evaluation on what you think would be suitable for your particular child. How's his memory retention? Does he assimilate ideas more when a lesson is read or if he reads it himself? Knowing this will help you determine your child's specific needs, and even the right approach to learning.

2. Set a planning day.

On this day, you will evaluate your child's weekly performance, including their attitude. Check which method works best for your child, especially which subjects they are having a hard time with. This should be an open discussion, and will allow you to determine where you need to focus more, and where more advanced learning can take place.

3.   Plan your lessons well

Determine which lessons can be accomplished easily and which will need more help with. Set learning goals for the year or semester, such as learn Pythagoras theorem. Then you can set weekly lessons and goals to work towards this ultimate goal.

By planning a more practical goal, you can easily set your weekly schedule and activities. This may include memorizing a poem, the table of elements, or a formula.

4.   Organize your room according to your present needs.

It's important that the study room is not a distracting place. For each separate lesson, it can be best to remove all books and study material of other subjects. Try and keep your child focused on the task at hand.

5.   Set your to-do list.

As you go through homeschooling, you need to routinely set your to-do list. This includes house-chores and even your job. All of these will be affected once you start homeschooling your child, and it's imperative that you can handle your time well.

Chapter 4: Setting Up Your Study Space

Considering a space where you and your child can study together may be important, but don't get stuck on the idea you need an extra room for it. While having a different room can be helpful, it's not necessary and many families do not use one.

Some families do school work together right on their dining table. You may even find some kids, who are homeschooling, working someplace else outside of home. It doesn't really matter whether you have a spare room or an empty corner where your child can study. What matters is that they have a space where they can study and where items they can use are kept.

Factors to Consider in Setting Your Study Space

Before you plan on considering a space or deciding to use the kitchen table for a while, there are things you need to consider.

Distractions

In creating a space where your child will study you need to consider the distractions. This doesn't just include the television or their toys. Even other activities done inside the house can be distracting.

If you plan to use the dining area as your study desk, your family's eating time can be a distraction, especially if your child is in the middle of a school work. When a child is concentrating and you want his things removed from the dining table for a while to set the table for lunch or dinner, it breaks their momentum.

Another form of distraction is toys. It's not wise to have your child's toys stored near their study area, especially if you are using a separate room. Keep these away from their reach during study time.

Be aware of what can distract your child's focus on their school work.

Good lighting

You want your child to study well? Consider having a study area where they can enjoy natural lighting. It helps children read more and will take care of their eye sight.

Organizing learning supplies

Learning supplies such as books and notebooks, even pens, art paper, pencils, and crayons, should be stored neatly. Know what items your child needs most of the time. Invest in some shelves and boxes where they can keep them after using.

Whether you've decided to use the dining area, or someplace near it, you need to focus on creating the best environment possible for your child.

Creating Your Space

Setting up your homeschool space is easy after knowing where to have it. Whether it's temporary or not, here are some reminders to help make your space perfect for learning.

1. Make your study space livable.

Have a study space where your child can work comfortably. It should have enough room for both of you to move. You should also consider the tables you will be placing in and if you want shelves too.

The space should also be cozy. It also shouldn't be too cold or hot.

2. Invest in desks and chairs.

While you can use your dining table for study, it pays to invest in some good quality desks and chairs for your homeschool. It may seem like an unnecessary expense now, but if you plan on homeschooling your child for several years, it is a very smart investment.

3. Include technology in your homeschool space.

A lot of parents may consider computers to be very distracting, but its benefits to learning are undeniable. You can opt for security measures with your child's usage by limiting the websites he can visit (or blocking some distracting websites). A laptop is ideal because you can remove it from the space depending on what your child is working on, and if they require it.

4. Take an inventory of your items.

Your child will be studying at home. This means there's a chance you may find a crayon or two far from his study space, or his math workbook in the living room or the backyard.

Take note of the items your child uses. This will give you a good idea of what's missing and what needs replacements.

Facilitating your Home Learning

Facilitating learning is not limited to a certain space or room where your child is studying. In homeschooling, you need to have your whole home transformed to a learning-friendly zone. You can have all school items in one place to keep it organized. You may, also, have books and other work in different areas depending on the space you have available.

Some kids don't limit their study time in their own space. There are those who do their math homework on the trampoline, or elsewhere. Having every area of your home ready for homeschool learning is essential.

Chapter 5: Making Time to Homeschool

Your time needs to be adjusted when it comes to attending to your child's homeschool needs. As was said in the previous chapters, deciding to homeschool is not easy. You need to sacrifice certain activities to be there for your child. Even regular day to day tasks like your cleaning and cooking can be compromised.

In making time for homeschool there are three areas you need to consider: your time, your child's time, and your time together. This is not just about your time together since you both have certain tasks to meet. Your child may need to meet up with friends, play, or even do math problems and study on their own. You, on the other hand, have your responsibilities in managing the whole house (especially if you have work).

Your Time

Making time to homeschool requires you to adjust your schedule. This means you have to divide your time between your housework, your job, your family, and your role as your child's teacher.

There will be times when certain tasks such as cleaning will need to be put on hold when your child needs more assistance. You may need to consider hiring house cleaning services or arrange your house in a way that it's easy to keep it tidy.

You also have your role as a parent and as a spouse. This may mean attending to your other children's needs, especially if you have a baby or small children. You may include your other children in helping their sibling. You may even have to adjust your homeschooling schedule to four times a week to make room for other family matters.

As your child's teacher you need to have time not just to review but also to evaluate your child's performance. You also need to attend conferences and meetings to help arrange activities your child can enjoy with other homeschooled children.

Working Together

Homeschool gives you an opportunity to spend time with your child. It can help you both create a closer bond as you see through their progress. You also get a chance to include certain topics and activities which are not usually offered in a regular class. Possible subjects you can include and which you and your child can discuss with the whole family are bible study, nature study and art and music appreciation.

If your child is learning how to read, the whole family can help out by having time to help them read out loud. You can also allocate time to memorize poems to practice dictation.

Teaching the Child to Work Independently

There will be instances when your child needs to do their school work alone. Teaching them to work independently may take some time, especially if they are used to having you assist them every time.

The transition from working together to working independently also has its rewards. They learn to be responsible and to even manage their own time.

To help them work independently, you can set a schedule where you both can work together on a certain task. This is where you assist them. Slowly let your child work through your planned activity while you oversee their work. After sometime, slowly let your child do the work alone with a given time allowance. You may give them a writing composition task or a math problem to solve on their own for one hour. While they do this, you can do other tasks such as cooking or your laundry. When the time is up, your child can place his work where all accomplished tasks are kept for your checking.

Organizing learning items really helps. Having a basket where your child can place the assignments you give them once completed is a good idea. Then you can check them in your own time. Here are some activities your child can do alone.

- Math problems
- Copywork
- Assigned activities from a book
- Computer activities
- Picture study
- Science observation activities
- Reading

As you slowly let your child learn how to do work independently, you are able to adjust your schedule to work on other task as they accomplish theirs.

Chapter 6: Experiencing Homeschooling Success

What else do you need to know in order to succeed in homeschooling your child?

Deciding to homeschool your child requires you to evaluate yourself: your resources, time, and even your attitude to work things out. The decision may seem difficult, especially as you are just starting the whole process, but it can be worthwhile in the end. You get to discover your child's prowess, help them develop, and have a closer bond with them and with the whole family.

Characteristics to Develop as a Homeschool Teacher

Making a venture successful requires you to develop certain traits. This will determine your success and how far you will go. To help you succeed in homeschooling, here are traits you need to develop.

Eagerness to learn more

As you teach your child, you also get to learn. Before you can present a lesson, you need to review the information, and make sure you understand it yourself. It may take your time off certain activities but learning can be very fun. It can be rewarding to be learning at the same time as your child.

Effort

Every endeavor that's worth working out needs effort. You need to work hard to really succeed in your homeschooling venture with your child. It needs to be approached as a job, and requires similar commitment.

Discipline

Since a lot of your time will be taken by homeschool activities, you need to develop discipline in following your schedule. This will help you work out your tasks effectively. You don't have to rush on things, but you need to provide your child the attention they need.

Patience

Patience is highly required especially when teaching children. There will be times your child doesn't want to study and would prefer playing. You may even meet tantrums along the way. There's also frustration if you see them excel at something, and stops putting effort it. You need patience to understand your child and guide them best.

Adventurous

You need to be adventurous to learn new and exciting things. As you homeschool your child, you need to assess, plan, and adjust as you meet unexpected events.

Informing the School

Informing the school of your decision to homeschool your child can be intimidating. You are entering a world of professionally trained teachers to tell them that you will be your child's teacher from now on. While there are institutions that may discourage you, there are some which will encourage you too. They may have noticed the child's need to be with their parent more and will recommend being educated from home. There are instances his teachers may offer help.

Don't feel intimidated in facing them. You need to compose yourself and be confident that you are going to do a good job.

Tracking Your Child's Progress

Recording your child's progress is essential in determining the next steps you are to take in their learning. This is what your next year's homeschool plan will be based on. You can easily keep tabs on your child progress by assessing each of their subject's progress, their character, and other thoughts or areas which you believe may seem useful.

Homeschooling is not just about making sure that academics develop further. It is also about shaping a child's character. The best way for your child to learn this is through you teaching by example. The discipline, dedication, and patients you show can help your child see and assimilate the characteristics you want them to have.

Tracking development can also be accomplished with the help of other parents with homeschooled children. You can exchange views and even be able to share ideas on how to hone your child's skills more. You can plan activities where you all get to spend time together.

If you think you will have a difficult time teaching high level subjects, then you can hire a tutor. You can ask them to report their assessment of your child's progress to you. You also get to them work through the curriculum. This is another way of letting your child discover their potential further and not grow dependent on you. They get to work with another adult other than a parent. It may even help your child with social growth. Alternatively, perhaps you have chosen to homeschool because your child was struggling at a certain age. As your child grows, they may decide they are ready for regular school. Be open to this if your child is serious about it. If things don't work out, you can always go back to homeschooling!

Homeschooling is fun! It has a lot of positive impact on both the parents and child, especially in strengthening their relationship. Just remember that even with all the challenges this action may bring, have fun! The rewards are worth every sacrifice you need to make.

Conclusion

Thank you again for downloading this book!

I hope this book was able to help you learn more about homeschooling, and whether it is right for you.

The next step is to put this information to use, decide whether you want to homeschool, and begin!

Remember to carefully plan, and ensure you are ready before you begin. This is a big commitment, and it requires a lot of time and thought.

Good luck with your homeschooling journey, I wish you all the best and hope this book will be of some service to you!

Finally, if you enjoyed this book, please take the time to share your thoughts and post a review on Amazon. It'd be greatly appreciated!

Thank you and good luck!